W9-BLO-048

DECLARATION

•

I hereby declare that
all the paper produced
by Cartiere del Garda S.p.A.
in its Riva del Garda mill
is manufactured completely
<u>Acid-free and Wood-free</u>

Alois Lueftinger

Dr. Alois Lueftinger
Managing Director and General Manager
Cartiere del Garda S.p.A.

FUNGI AND LICHENS

Written by
Wendy Madgwick

STECK-VAUGHN
LIBRARY
A Division of Steck-Vaughn Company

Austin, Texas

**Published in the United States in 1990
by Steck-Vaughn, Co., Austin, Texas,**
a subsidiary of National Education Corporation

A Templar Book
Devised and produced by The Templar Company plc
Pippbrook Mill, London Road, Dorking, Surrey RH4 1JE, Great Britain
Copyright © 1990 by The Templar Company plc

Editor: Wendy Madgwick
Designer: Jane Hunt
Illustrator: Jane Pickering
Scientific adviser: Joy Fildes

Notes to Reader
There are some words in this book that are printed in **bold** type.
A brief explanation of these words is given in the glossary on p. 44.

All living things are given two Latin names when first classified by a
scientist. Some of them also have a common name, for example
fly agaric, *Amanita muscaria.* In this book, the common name is used where
possible, but the scientific name is given when first mentioned.

The plural of some words is different from the singular, for example fungus
(singular), fungi (plural). Both forms are given in the glossary.

Library of Congress Cataloging-in-Publication Data
Madgwick, Wendy, 1946–
Fungi and lichens / by Wendy Madgwick.   p. cm. – (The Green World)
"A Templar Book" – T.p. verso.   Includes bibliographical references.
Summary: Surveys the world of fungi and lichens, discussing such aspects as
fungi and decay, parasites, pollution, plant partnerships, edible and
poisonous fungi, and antibiotics.
ISBN 0-8114-2728-5
1. Fungi – Juvenile literature.   2. Lichens – Juvenile literature.
[1. Fungi.   2. Lichens.]   I. Title.   II. Series.
QK603.5.M36   1990   90-9571
589.2–dc20   CIP AC

Color separations by Positive Colour Ltd, Maldon, Essex, Great Britain
Printed and bound by L.E.G.O., Vicenza, Italy
2 3 4 5 6 7 8 9 0 LE 94 93

Photographic credits
t = top, b = bottom, l = left, r = right
Cover: Bruce Coleman; page 9 Alan Wheals, Bath University; page 10
Frank Lane; page 12 Forestry Commission; page 13 Frank Lane/Holt
Studios; page 14 Frank Lane/Holt Studios; page 15 ICI Agrochemicals;
page 17 Frank Lane; page 19*l* Bruce Coleman/Peter Ward; page 19*r* Bruce
Coleman/Adrian Davies; page 21*l* Frank Lane/Holt Studios; page 21*r*
Frank Lane/Steve McCutcheon; page 22 Bruce Coleman/Hans Reinhard;
page 24 Frank Lane/Holt Studios; page 26 Frank Lane/Holt Studios;
page 27 Popperfoto; page 31 Bruce Coleman/Hans Reinhard; page37
Bruce Coleman/Peter Ward; page 38*l, r* ICI Agrochemicals; page 39*l*
Confédération Générale de Roquefort; page 39*r* Forestry Commission;
page 40 Rentokil; page 41 Mushroom Growers Association.

CONTENTS

GREEN WORLD

This tree shows the different groups of plants and fungi that are found in the world. It does not show how they developed or their relationship with each other.

Lichens
- Permanent association between a fungus and an alga (single-celled green plant)
- Cannot live in the dark or in polluted air

Basidiomycetes
- Dropping-spore fungi
- Spores form on a special cell called a basidium

Ascomycetes
- Shooting-spore fungi
- Spores form in a special tube or bag called an ascus

Fungi imperfecti
- Only produce short-lived or asexual spores
- Many live in the soil

Phycomycetes
- Mostly exploding-spore fungi
- A collection of unrelated fungi

Fungi
- Do not contain chlorophyll (green pigment)
- Feed on living or dead animals and plants

Slime molds
- These are not true fungi
- Do not form hyphae or threads

CONIFEROUS (OR FIR) TREES (Gymnosperms)

FLOWERING PLANTS (Angiosperms)

FERNS, CLUB MOSSES, AND HORSETAILS (Pteridophytes)

MOSSES AND LIVERWORTS (Bryophytes)

ALGAE

GREEN PLANTS

ANIMALS

PLANTS

FUNGI AND LICHENS

BACTERIA

LIVING THINGS

The land area of the world is divided into ten main zones depending on the plants that grow there. Fungi are found throughout the world, except in the very cold Antarctic and very dry deserts.

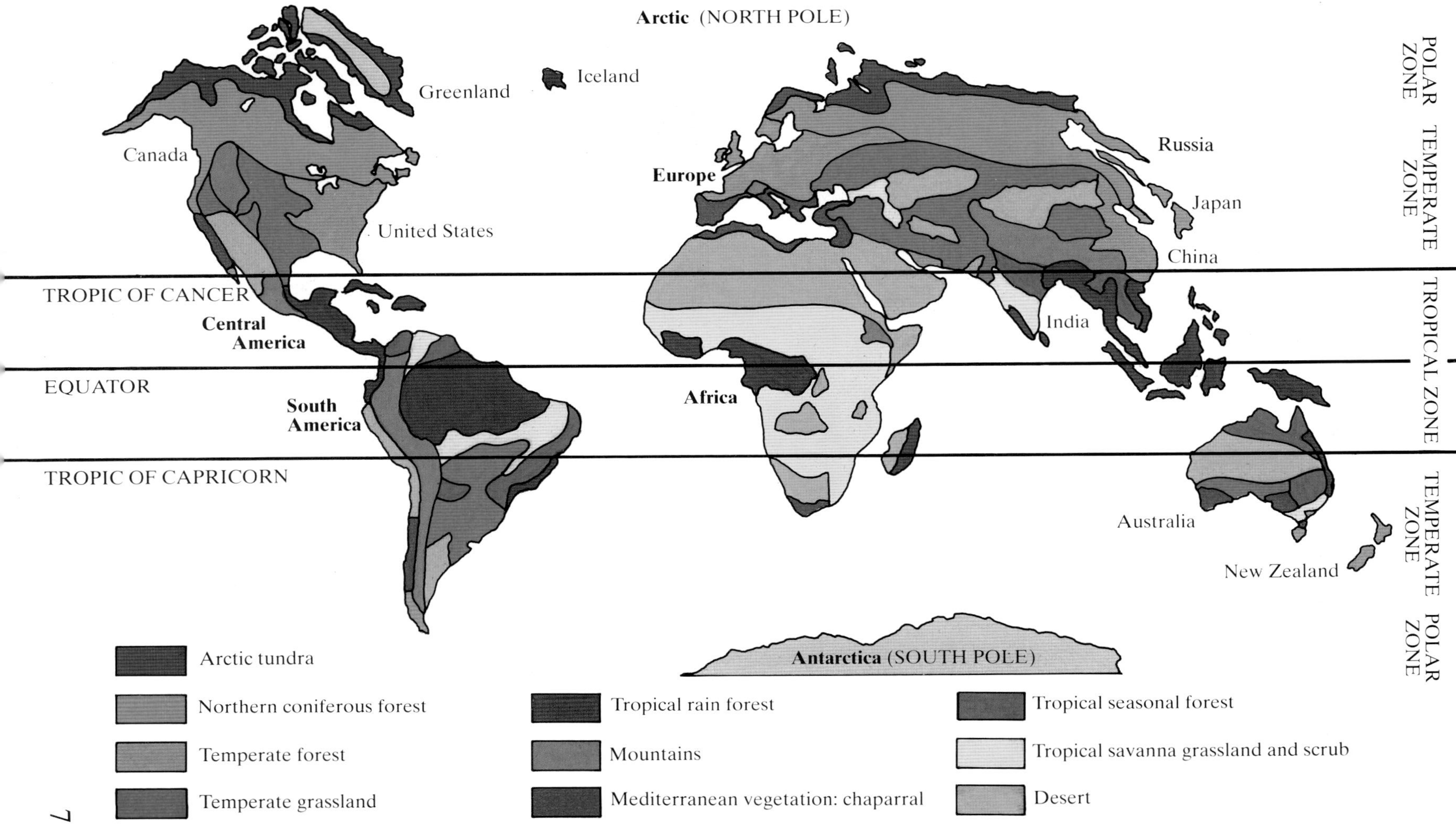

POLAR ZONE   TEMPERATE ZONE   TROPICAL ZONE   TEMPERATE ZONE   POLAR ZONE

Russia

Japan

China

India

New Zealand

Australia

Arctic (NORTH POLE)

Europe

Africa

Iceland

Greenland

United States

Central America

South America

Canada

TROPIC OF CANCER

EQUATOR

TROPIC OF CAPRICORN

Antarctica (SOUTH POLE)

Tropical rain forest

Mountains

Mediterranean vegetation: chaparral

Tropical seasonal forest

Tropical savanna grassland and scrub

Desert

Arctic tundra

Northern coniferous forest

Temperate forest

Temperate grassland

7

FUNGI

Fungi come in all shapes and sizes. Mushrooms and toadstools are well-known kinds, but there are many others. Many fungi are so small that they cannot be seen with the naked eye. Others like the giant puffballs and the Australian *Boletus portenosus* may be over 18 inches wide.

Most fungi begin life as a **spore,** which, like the seed of plants, will grow into a new fungus. From the spore, one thread, or **hypha**, will grow and divide into two. In time hundreds of threads, or hyphae, will grow. These form the **feeding body**, or **mycelium**, of the fungus.

Below, you can see an example of a feeding body growing inside a fallen tree. The threads grow by feeding on the plant materials inside the tree. On the outside, there is often no sign that another **organism** (living thing) is inside the fallen tree. After feeding for some time, the feeding body develops a **fruiting body** (see p. 30). This is usually the only part of a fungus that we can see. Each fruiting body then goes on to produce millions of spores of its own. These are carried away by the wind to find a new food supply and so start the cycle again.

Some fungi feed on living animals, for example, fungi can grow on the gills of fish or on human feet (see p. 16). Others feed on dead material – the mold that grows on clothes or bread, for instance. Many form a partnership with **algae**, tiny green plants, to form lichens (see p. 18), and others form a relationship with the roots of plants (see pp. 22-25).

Spores from an oyster mushroom, *Pleurotus ostreatus*, are carried by the wind to land on the trunk of a fallen tree. Each spore can only be seen with the aid of a microscope, but when many thousands are deposited together, they can be seen with the naked eye.

The threads of the feeding body develop from the spores and spread outward throughout the tree trunk. The threads grow only inside the log.

Molds

The fungal mold that grows on stale bread fills the loaf with threadwork, which digests the bread before producing pin-head spores. The individual fruiting bodies are so small that they can only be seen with a magnifying glass.

When conditions are right, the fruiting body develops. This will produce a new generation of spores to be dispersed by the wind.

Single cells

Unusual fungi like the **yeasts**, which we use to make bread, do not form threads. If there is enough food, each yeast cell will produce a small bud that will grow to form another cell and so on until a large group of cells is formed.

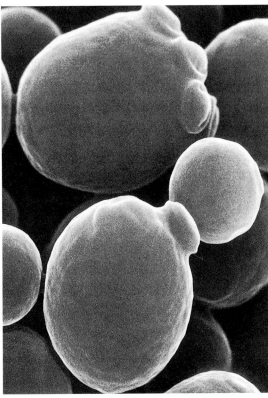

- Although fungi have been called plants in the past, they are neither plants nor animals; they are in a kingdom of their own.
- There are at least 65,000 species of fungi.
- Fungi do not contain **chlorophyll** (green pigment) so they cannot make food in the way that plants can (see p. 18).
- Fungi can feed on anything which is, or has been, alive.
- Fungi and **bacteria** (microscopic organisms) prevent the natural world from having unwanted waste by decaying and recycling dead plants and animals.
- Fungi live everywhere, except in regions where it is too cold, or too dry.

FUNGI AND DECAY

There are at least 65,000 kinds of fungi known at present, and there may well be many more. Perhaps this enormous number indicates their importance in the natural world. One of their most valuable functions, along with bacteria, is to break down or decay dead animals and plants. If there were no fungi in the world, fields and woods would soon be knee-deep in fallen leaves and the forests full of fallen trees. Although bacteria help in the process of decay, fungi are far more important. Organisms that live on dead plant and animal remains are called **saprophytes**.

Fungi use some of the food to grow, but they return a lot of the nutrients, or food products, to the soil where they are used by growing plants. Many fungi that live in the soil are saprophytes. The threads grow out in a ring from the center of the food source and the fruiting bodies, for example toadstools, form on the outer edge making a fairy ring. The activity of the fungus makes the soil rich in nitrogen so that the grass grows well and looks darker than the surrounding vegetation.

The molds that you sometimes find in your home growing on food, clothes, paper, leather, and similar goods are all saprophytic fungi. The molds can live on these things because they are all made from plant and animal products.

Beautiful poisoner
The verdigris agaric, *Stropharia aeruginosa*, is found in woods and pastures. It is probably a saprophyte and has been found growing on dead tree trunks or stumps, leaves, and dung. It is poisonous, but is usually not deadly.

Breaking down dung

Dung, such as cowpats, is decayed in a similar way to leaves. Many fungi grow on dung. One of the first to attack the dung is a tiny species of *Pilobus*. When *Pilobus* has absorbed enough food, it forms spores in a spore capsule. The capsule takes in water and explodes, shooting the spores out. The spores land on the grass and are eaten by a cow. They pass through the cow's gut and are deposited, with the dung, onto a new site, and the cycle starts again. These fungi are followed by the air-borne spores of the cup-shaped *Peziza* fungi, which in turn are followed by toadstools, for example the ink cap, *Coprinus niveus*. Finally all the dung is decayed. Many of the nutrients, especially minerals like nitrates and phosphates that are essential for plant growth, have been returned to the soil.

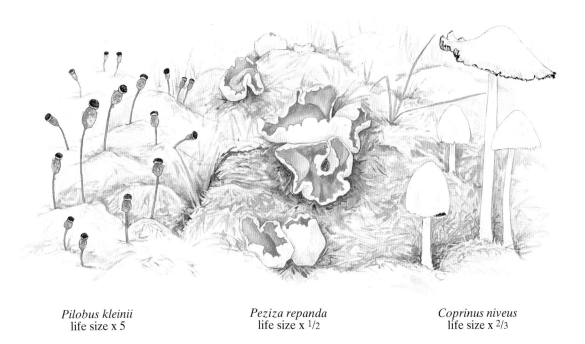

Pilobus kleinii
life size x 5

Peziza repanda
life size x 1/2

Coprinus niveus
life size x 2/3

How saprophytic fungi get their food

Fungi take in their food through the cell walls of the feeding body, and so the threads have to be in close contact with the food. The threads produce special chemicals, called **enzymes**, which can break down, or digest, animal and plant cells. The enzymes pass out of the fungal cells (arrow 1) into the dead material, in this case dead leaves. Here the enzymes break down the leaf cells into simple substances, such as the sugars glucose and sucrose. These chemicals are small enough to pass through the wall of the fungus (arrow 2), which uses them as food, to grow and produce spores and fruiting bodies.

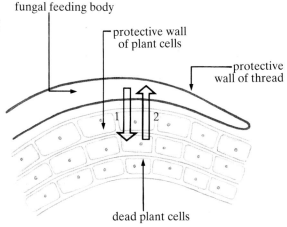

fungal feeding body

protective wall
of plant cells

protective
wall of thread

dead plant cells

11

PARASITES OF PLANTS

Most fungi live on dead plants or animals, but some are **parasites** and feed on living things. For example, white powdery mildews and reddish-brown rusts can be seen on the leaves of many living trees and shrubs. These small fungi damage the leaves so that they lose water and the plant slowly wilts and dies. A few of the fungi that live in the soil are parasites. Some attack, and eventually kill, seeds or young seedlings, while others live on the roots of plants.

The effect of mold and fungal attack can be seen in many woods and forests. Each year some trees die from the damage caused by fungi. Some fungi, such as the birch polypore, *Piptoporus betulinus*, grow only on one type of tree. Others, for example the honey fungus, *Armillaria mellea*, will grow on many different kinds of tree. Some land on the tree as spores, and their threads grow through the leaves or cracks in the bark and spread throughout the tree. Others grow up through the roots into the tree trunk. The fungi continue to grow until all the food source is used up and the tree is dead. Then they produce fruiting bodies that release spores to start the cycle over again.

Dutch Elm Disease

A line of dead elm trees is a common sight in the northern hemisphere (see map on p. 7). The cause is usually a fungus, called Dutch elm disease. The disease is carried from one elm to another by the elm bark beetle. As the beetle tunnels under the bark to lay its eggs, the fungal spores carried on its body are deposited in the tree.

The fungus spreads throughout the tree, destroying the living tissue. Eventually it reaches the roots and invades them. As the fungus grows, it makes many small yeast-like bodies. These are carried along the **xylem**, the tubes in the plant that carry water. These tubes become blocked so that water cannot get through. The leaves turn yellow and the branch slowly dies from lack of water. More and more branches die until finally the whole tree is dead.

Honey fungus

The honey fungus gets its name from its honey-colored top surface. The threads of this fungus cling together to form thick, black "bootlace" strands called **rhizomorphs**, which grow up inside the bark. They also grow in the soil from one tree to the next. The disease is incurable and the tree eventually dies. Affected trees are often burned to prevent infection of nearby trees.

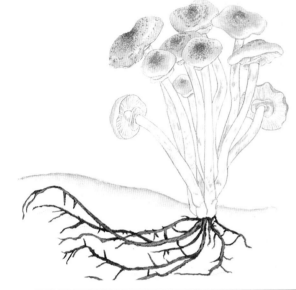

Bracket fungus

Many large birch trees have a bracket fungus growing somewhere on their trunks. This one, called the birch polypore, is the fruiting body of a fungus that has been feeding on the birch tree for some time. By the time they are 40 years old, most birch trees will have died from such an attack. Many other trees in the forest live to be well over 100 years old, so birch trees die young.

PESTS OF CROPS

Many of the most destructive diseases of cultivated plants, for example the smuts and rusts of cereals, potato blight, and mildews, are caused by very small fungi. The gray molds that you see on soft fruits like strawberries are due to *Botrytus* fungi. The lumpy blisters sometimes seen on the leaves of pear trees and the silver leaf disease of plum trees are caused by fungi. Silver leaf disease is so serious a pest, destroying whole orchards, that the authorities have to be told of an outbreak.

Crops can be protected by spraying them with chemicals. Hops (plants used to make beer) infected with downy mildew disease, *Pseudoperanospera humuli*, are often sprayed with an **antibiotic** called streptomycin (see p. 26). This antibiotic is made by a fungus called *Streptomyces griseus*.

Cultivated plants are grown close together – ideal conditions for the growth of any pest. The fungi spread from one plant to the next very easily, destroying the crop and causing a great deal of food to be lost.

Potato blight
Potato blight, *Phytophthora infestans*, attacks the leaves (see below) and is the potato farmers' worst enemy. It spreads rapidly, destroying whole crops. In the mid-nineteenth century, this fungus caused great damage throughout Europe, especially in Ireland. The destruction of the potato crop caused a famine, and thousands of people starved to death.

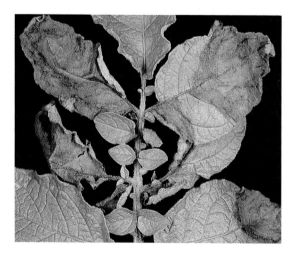

Poisonous molds
Some molds not only destroy crops, they also produce poisonous chemicals. Nuts and grains kept in mild (above 52°F), damp conditions may become infected with *Aspergillus flavus*. The fungus produces a poison called aflatoxin. If the infected nuts or grain are eaten, the liver can be damaged and the animal may die.

Rusts and smuts

Grain crops, for example wheat, barley, rye, sweet corn, and rice, sometimes grow black or reddish-brown spots or patches (see below). These are caused by rust and smut fungi, which have unusual and complicated life cycles. The fungi often spend the winter on another type of host plant growing near the crops. Some rusts use two kinds of host plants, living on them every other winter. The black rust of wheat, *Puccinia graminis*, spends the winter on the barberry, and during its life it produces five different kinds of spores. This disease has caused millions of tons worth of damage in both North America and Australia. Strains of wheat that cannot be attacked by the fungus have been bred, but the fungus can adapt and infect the new strain. Over 200 types of black rust have been identified. The best way to combat the disease is to remove the other host plants from the area in which the crop is growing.

Saint Anthony's fire

Grasses and the cereal rye are occasionally infected with ergot fungus, *Claviceps purpurea*. This fungus infects the flowers, producing a small, hard, dark, banana-shaped body (see above). This structure, called the ergot, is full of spores. If the infected plant is harvested and ground up, the flour will be poisoned. When it is eaten as bread, it causes severe pain with burning feelings, called Saint Anthony's fire. Large doses can lead to death. A chemical called ergotamine, which is made from ergot, is used by doctors. Very small doses are given to patients to cause muscles to tighten or contract. It is particularly helpful in childbirth.

PARASITES OF ANIMALS

Many animals, including humans, can suffer from fungal infections. Fungi that grow as parasites on animals often live in the surface layers of the skin. They do not normally kill their hosts, but they can cause pain and look very unpleasant.

Many people suffer from a fungal infection at some time. Athlete's foot is found on the skin between the toes. At first, the fungus lives on dead skin, but it soon enters the living cells, causing pain. "Ringworm" attacks the scalp and other parts of the body, making the hair fall out and leaving round bald spots. Both athlete's foot and ringworm are caused by fungi from three groups, *Trichophyton*, *Microsporum*, and *Epidermophyton*.

Many animals, for example rabbits and mice, breathe in the spores of heat-loving fungi, which live in warm places like compost heaps. These fungi are normally saprophytes (see p. 10), but when they grow in the lungs, they act as parasites causing lung diseases, which may end in death. In people, the dry rot fungus, *Serpula lacrymans*, can cause asthma if breathed in, and a chest infection known as "farmer's lung" is caused by spores released from moldy hay.

White moldy patches can often be seen on the fins and scales of fish. Some fungi penetrate into the fish's body, killing it. The mold *Saprolegnia* usually grows on dead fish, but it will attack and destroy the eggs of live fish as well.

Staggering flies

Flies are attacked by the fungus called *Entomophthora muscae*. The flies lose their sense of balance, staggering around before they die. Their bodies become covered with the white spores of the fungus. Other flies that come to explore the dead body pick up the spores and suffer the same fate.

Super glue

A fungus that lives in freshwater ponds catches its food in a very unusual way. Lollipop-shaped knobs develop on the fungal threads. These attract tiny fast-swimming creatures called rotifers. The rotifer tries to eat the knob, and becomes stuck. There is no escape, and the fungus invades and feeds on its prey.

A clever snare

Some fungi use unbelievable methods to catch their animal food. *Dactyella bembicodes*, which lives in the soil, grows a ring-shaped structure just like a snare. When the tiny nematode worm wriggles into the ring, the ring swells up, holding the worm so tightly that it cannot escape. The threads then grow into the worm, feeding on it.

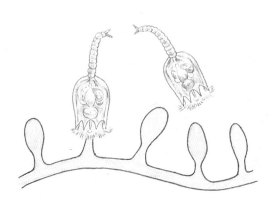

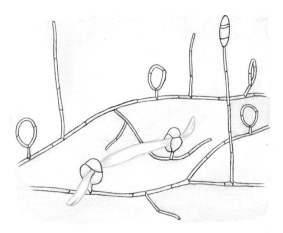

Caterpillars under attack

Cordyceps militaris, the scarlet caterpillar fungus, feeds on the caterpillars of moths and butterflies as they lie **dormant** (resting) underground.

Sometimes it is the **pupa**, the stage between caterpillar and adult, that is attacked. The fungus feeds on the bodies and then makes a fruiting body, which grows above ground.

LICHENS

Many fungi can live on or with plants without killing them. When two living organisms (plant, animal, or fungus) live together with some benefit for each partner, we call it a **symbiotic** relationship. Fungi form two kinds of partnerships, one with the roots of trees and other higher plants, called **mycorrhizae** (see p. 22), and one with algae, called lichens.

Lichens are formed from a fungus and a microscopic green plant called an alga. The algae actually live between the fungal threads. The algal cells are green because they contain the green pigment chlorophyll. Plants use this pigment to make their own food from water and a gas, carbon dioxide, using the energy of sunlight. This process is called **photosynthesis**. The fungus receives all its food from the algae and in return the fungus gives the algae some protection from drying out and from too much ultraviolet light.

It is not known which partner makes the pigments found in lichens, but they are at the surface where they will offer most protection against sunlight. These pigments give the lichens their distinctive colors: orange and yellow; white and pale gray; black and dark browns; and grayish green.

All the algae found in lichens could exist on their own, although only in darker, wetter places. However, none of the fungi found in lichens can exist on their own. Also, only the fungus produces spores; the alga does not seem to have enough energy left to do this after "feeding" the fungus. So the relationship seems slightly one-sided, and the fungus probably benefits more than the alga.

Structure of a lichen
This cross-section of a lichen shows how the algae live within the threads of the fungus.

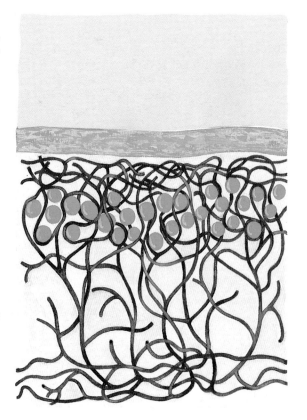

Shapes of lichens

Lichens come in three forms or shapes. Crustose lichens form flat, crusty plates which are stuck so tightly to the rocky surface that they are very difficult to remove. Foliose lichens are leafy, and the upper surface is often a different color from the lower one. Fruticose lichens form shrubby "branches" like miniature trees.

■ Lichens are formed from an association between a fungus and an alga.
■ There are about 15,000 lichens.
■ Lichens, unlike fungi, need light and cannot live in the dark.
■ Many lichens can grow only in clean, unpolluted air.
■ Lichens come in three shapes: flat crustose lichens, leafy foliose lichens, and branching fruticose lichens.

foliose lichen

fruticose lichen

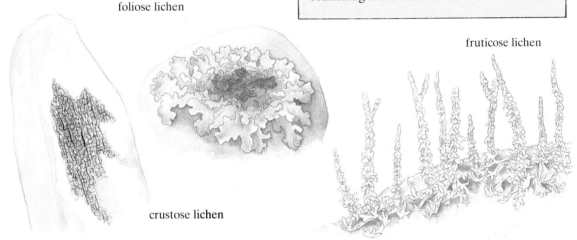

crustose lichen

Woodland sites

If you walk through open woodland you will see many lichens like the stag's horn, *Evernia prunastri*, growing on tree trunks. Lichens do not damage the plants on which they grow.

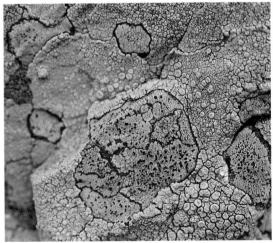

Light, not dark

Lichens, like green plants, need to live in fairly light places. Therefore lichens do not live in the soil or in wood. Instead they live on the outside of bare rocks and on the branches and trunks of trees. *Rhizocarpon geographicum*, the map lichen shown above, is often found on rocks.

LICHENS AND POLLUTION

Most lichens can only grow in clean air. They cannot survive in towns and cities where exhaust fumes and smoke from chimneys and factories have polluted the air. As many lichens grow on rocks and stones, a good place to find them is in a churchyard. Often the gravestones are covered with lichens, forming a living paint. In an area with pure, clean air as many as 20 kinds of lichen may grow on a limestone gravestone and as many as 40 on a sandstone one.

There are many kinds of "dirt" in the air. Sulfur dioxide, a gas, is one kind and it is invisible. This gas will dissolve in water to form an acid. It will dissolve in the rain as it falls. The more of this gas there is in the air, the more acid the rain will be. Acid rain slowly destroys many plants and trees as well as lichens.

The growth of certain lichens can be used to test how pure the air is in a particular area and a pollution chart can be drawn.

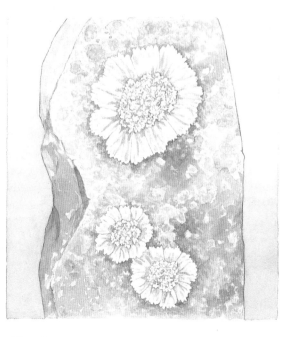

Keeping a partner
Many lichens produce small powdery lumps, called soredia, on their surface. These contain both algal cells and fungal threads. When they are blown away or carried by insects to another area, the lichen is ready to grow again.

Pollution chart
Some lichens can live in dirtier air than others, and those shown here are typical examples of lichens found in the different pollution zones. Those that grow in one zone can, of course, grow in less-polluted areas.

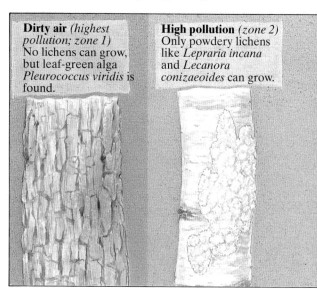

Dirty air (*highest pollution; zone 1*)
No lichens can grow, but leaf-green alga *Pleurococcus viridis* is found.

High pollution (*zone 2*)
Only powdery lichens like *Lepraria incana* and *Lecanora conizaeoides* can grow.

Finding the right partner

At certain times, the fungus in the lichen produces spores from a variety of differently shaped fruiting bodies. Some look like tiny volcanoes, and others like jelly cookies. When the fruiting bodies are ripe, the spores are released. It is not known how the fungal spores find the right algal cell to reform the lichen.

Lichens and people

Lichens are used by people in many ways. **Indicators**, which show how acid something is, can be made from lichens. For example, the indicator litmus is made from *Roccella* species. In Norway, Sweden, and Iceland, lichens are sometimes used to make colored dyes. Unfortunately, vast amounts of the lichen are needed to make even a small amount of dye, and so many lichens are being destroyed. In winter, the Saami in Scandinavia feed their deer on reindeer moss (*Cladonia rangiferina*; shown above) and Iceland moss *(Cetraria islandica)*.

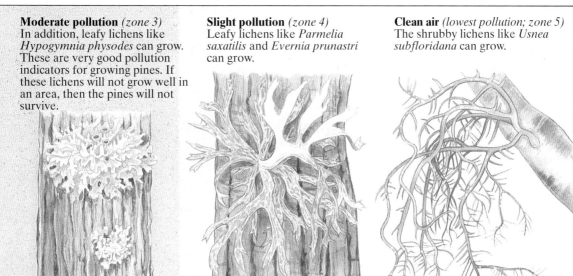

Moderate pollution *(zone 3)*
In addition, leafy lichens like *Hypogymnia physodes* can grow. These are very good pollution indicators for growing pines. If these lichens will not grow well in an area, then the pines will not survive.

Slight pollution *(zone 4)*
Leafy lichens like *Parmelia saxatilis* and *Evernia prunastri* can grow.

Clean air *(lowest pollution; zone 5)*
The shrubby lichens like *Usnea subfloridana* can grow.

PLANT PARTNERSHIPS

Many trees such as pine, oak, and birch are found in places with very poor soil but they still grow very well. A German scientist found that the root tips of these trees were surrounded by fungal threads. In some cases, the roots are covered in a mass of fine threadwork, but in others the threads invade the roots forming a network in the outer cells. The roots often appear to be fatter and shorter with more branches than usual. The fungi and the roots of the tree have formed a symbiotic relationship. Such associations, called mycorrhizae, are common in many woodlands, especially in temperate regions.

The fungus receives vitamins, simple proteins, and the sugars glucose and sucrose from the tree. Inside the fungus these sugars are changed into various forms of food and stored. Some of these stored foods, for example glycogen, are similar to those found in animals.

Pine partnerships

When *Pinus radiata*, the monterrey pine, was first planted in Australia, it did not grow well at all. Then a small amount of soil, with the right fungus, was added to the plantation. The pine began to grow much more quickly, and now there are thousands of tall, healthy trees. The fungi concerned are *Amanita muscaria* (the fly agaric), *Suillus luteus* (slippery jack), and *Suillus granulatus*.

What does the fungi give in return? It has been shown that certain minerals, for example phosphates, nitrates, and potassium, when in very short supply are more easily taken up by the fungus than the plant. Some fungi can store the phosphate and release it to the tree gradually as it needs it. Plants need these minerals in order to grow properly, and so this relationship is especially important in poor soils.

Types of mycorrhiza

When the fungal threads grow around and between the tree roots they form ectotrophic mycorrhizae. When the fungal threads actually grow inside the outer layer of the root they form endotrophic mycorrhizae. Pine, spruce, firs, larch, oak, beech, birch, sweet chestnut, hornbeam, and eucalyptus all form ectotrophic mycorrhizae. Many crops such as apples, strawberries, and tomatoes form endotrophic mycorrhizae. None of these plants grow as well without their fungal partners.

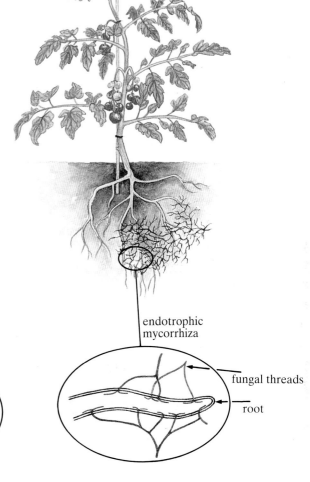

endotrophic
mycorrhiza

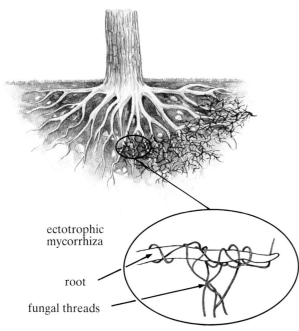

ectotrophic
mycorrhiza

root

fungal threads

fungal threads

root

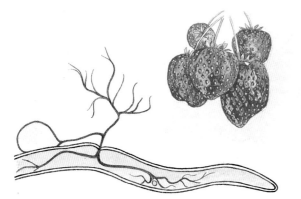

An ancient friend

Many endotrophic mycorrhizae are formed with the fungus *Endogone*, which seems to be best adapted for mycorrhizal life. Fungi that appear to be very similar have been found in the fossilized rootlike stems of fernlike plants growing in the Devonian period, some 350 million years ago.

Experiments in the U.S., U.K., Germany, and New Zealand have shown that plants like apple, strawberry, tobacco, corn, tomato, and the conifer podocarpus grow much better and have larger crops with the fungus than without it. Podocarpus grown with *Endogone* weighed just over six times as much as the trees without it.

FUNGI AND ORCHIDS

Orchids produce vast numbers of seeds, each one so small that it would weigh less than one microgram. (A microgram is one-millionth of one gram.) A seed as small as this cannot contain much food, and yet some orchids grow into very large plants which reach the top of forest trees. The seeds germinate (begin to grow) beneath the ground and the young plants often continue to grow below the surface of the soil. Plants can only make their own food by photosynthesis in the light (see p. 20), so where does the orchid plant get its food from? It seems that young orchid plants depend entirely on fungi for their food.

The fungus infects the orchid roots as they start to grow from the germinating seed. The fungal threads invade the root cell and form a coil inside it. After some time, the cells of the fungus swell up and begin to break down into food which the orchids can take up or **absorb**. Then the same root cell is invaded by another fungal thread and the process is repeated. By this means a young orchid plant can grow below ground for many years, obtaining all its food from the fungus. The fungus grows only in the outer cells of the orchid root. Other cells in the orchid produce chemicals to stop the growth of the fungus. No one is sure what benefit the fungus gets from this relationship.

The bird's nest orchid
Most orchids will eventually grow above the ground, produce leaves, and photosynthesize their own food, some of which may be passed on to the fungus. How far the fungus helps the orchid once it has leaves is not known. Orchids with plenty of green leaves probably need little help, whereas those with few green leaves will need more help. Those plants that never develop any leaves or chlorophyll, like the bird's nest orchid pictured here, are dependent on their fungal partners throughout their lives.

How orchids grow

The tiny orchid seed develops a root and a shoot. The fungus grows around the tiny root and grows into the cells. It provides the young plant with all of its food until the shoot grows above the ground and produces green leaves.

1. Orchid seed begins to germinate.

2. Rootlets form and the fungus grows around them.

3. Fungal threads invade the roots.

4. The shoot begins to grow.

5. Green leaves develop.

6. Full-grown orchid in flower.

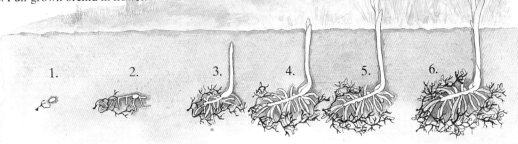

The orchid's friend

The honey fungus is often found as a parasite on trees and shrubs, causing a great deal of damage (see p. 13). It can, however, form a mycorrhizal partnership with many different kinds of orchids. The violet bird's nest orchid (*Limodorum abortivum*) pictured here is found in woods and on shady banks.

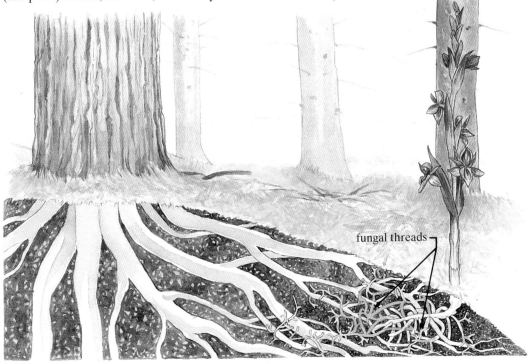

fungal threads

ENEMIES AND ANTIBIOTICS

Fungi are very hardy and have few enemies that can actually destroy them. Even the animals that attack them usually only kill the fruiting body and not the main feeding body. Many different kinds of animals, including humans, eat mushrooms and other fruiting bodies. Other animals, for example flies and beetles, lay their eggs inside the fruiting body, a ready source of food for the grubs when they hatch. Some trees and plants produce chemicals to stop the fungi from growing on them.

As with many animals and plants, competition for food and living space are the major concern of fungi. In this respect, other fungi and bacteria are their main rivals. Many fungi, for example *Streptomyces*, destroy their competitors, especially bacteria, by producing poisonous chemicals called antibiotics, which means "against life." Fortunately for us, these same chemicals have proved very useful medicines. Some yeasts like *Saccharomyces cerevisiae*, the yeast used in beer and wine making (see p. 38), have developed "killer" varieties. They produce poisons, or toxins, that kill other sensitive types of yeast. The so-called "wild" or natural types of yeasts are especially sensitive. These toxins may prove very useful in industry, preventing the growth of unwanted yeasts on food. They may also be useful in medicine since antibiotics that attack fungi are rare.

Some of the fungi that make mycorrhiza with trees (see p. 22) seem able to protect the tree from parasitic fungi. For example, if a tree has made a mycorrhiza with the fly agaric, then the parasitic honey fungus usually does not grow on it.

Fungus midges
These midges lay their eggs on fungi while the fruiting bodies of the fungi are very young. As the fruiting body grows, the eggs hatch and the grubs feed on its flesh. Their tiny burrowing holes can be seen very easily, as can the grubs.

Saving lives

In 1928, Sir Alexander Fleming discovered that a fungus, called *Penicillium notatum*, killed bacteria. He did many experiments and finally isolated a liquid, which he called penicillin, that would destroy many kinds of bacteria. It was greeted as a miracle cure and saved the lives of many wounded soldiers during World War II. Since then, many other antibiotics have been found. One, called streptomycin, is especially useful as it can be used to treat animals as well as humans. It can even be used to treat hops when they are suffering from downy mildew disease (another fungus).

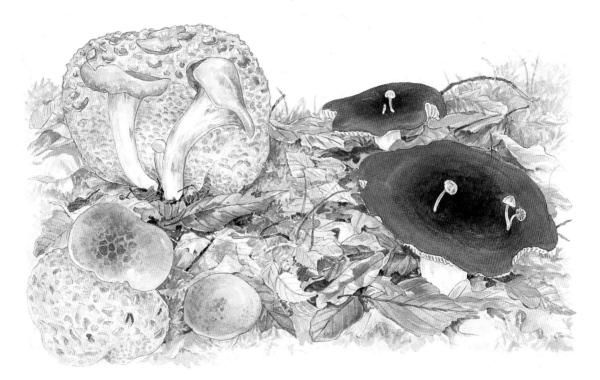

Like kills like

Some fungi are parasitic on other fungi. For example, *Boletus parasiticus* is often seen growing on the earth ball *Scleroderma*, and two *Asterophora* species are found growing on fungi like *Russula*.

27

SPORES AND CAPSULES

Most fungi reproduce, or make new fungi, by forming spores. Each spore is microscopic but, as thousands of them are shed at the same time, we see them as a fine dust or powder. Each kind of fungus produces spores of a particular shape, size, and color. They are so small and light that they can be blown long distances by the lightest of breezes. The spores are usually formed on or inside a spore container or a fruiting body. The feeding bodies of fungi look very alike, and so it is the kind of fruiting body and the type of spores produced that are used to divide the fungi into groups. **Mycologists**, people who study fungi, divide fungi into four groups and these will be described below and on the next page.

Most fungi produce two kinds of spores. One, a short-lived or asexual spore, is used to spread the fungus over the food supply. They only have to travel short distances and so need to live only for a short time.

When most of the food has been used up, some fungi produce permanent, or sexual, spores. These can survive for a long time and are often carried long distances. If the spore lands in a place where there is food, oxygen, and water, and it is not too cold, it will start to grow, and form a new feeding body (see p. 8).

Spore Prints

The spore containers of the imperfect fungi and phycomycetes shown on this page are very small, and cannot be used to make spore prints. However, on the next page you can see the large fruiting bodies of other fungi, and these can be used. Place the cap of the mushroom, gills downward, onto a sheet of paper or on sticky tape, which will stop the spores from moving. Leave it for a few hours, then carefully pick up the cap off the paper or sticky tape. The spores will have made a pattern that mirrors the position of the spores on the gills. If the spores are colorless you can use colored paper, or place the sticky tape onto colored paper. You could look at the spores through a magnifying glass or under a microscope.

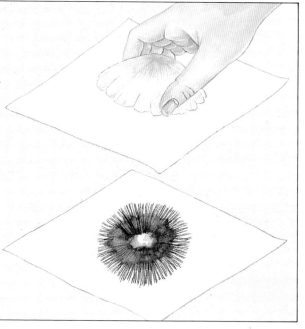

Exploding spore containers

Some of the smaller fungi make balloon-shaped spore containers, called **sporangia.** These containers, which are so small that you usually need a lens to see them, explode and scatter the spores on the surrounding food. These fungi also make sexual spores which are blown away to infect a new food supply. These small fungi, called spore-exploders or spore-floaters, belong to the group *Phycomycetes.* It is made up of a collection of about 11,000 kinds of unrelated fungi. Many of them are aquatic, living on dead water plants or animals. They produce spores that are adapted to float or move through the water. This group includes many molds, for example, bread mold and the fish mold *Saprolegnia,* as well as mildews, potato wart (*Synchytrium endobioticum*), and potato blight (*Phytophthora infestans*). The black bread mold (*Rhizopus stolonifera*) is pictured here.

Rhizopus stolonifera, black bread mold

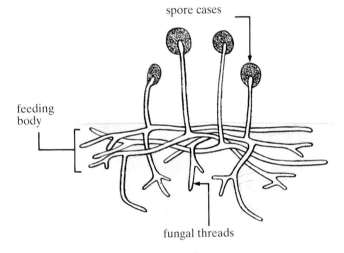

spore cases

feeding body

fungal threads

Imperfect fungi

(Fungi imperfecti)

The *Fungi imperfecti,* or *Deuteromycetes*, is made up of a collection of fungi. They have one major thing in common – they only produce asexual, or short-lived, spores. These often form as buds on the threads of the feeding body. They do not make sexual, or permanent, spores. There are about 11,000 different kinds, and many of them live in the soil. They include the soft gray *Botrytus* molds seen on rotting fruit, the *Fusarium* wilts found on potatoes and bananas and *Dactylella bembicodes,* which traps nematodes (see p. 17).

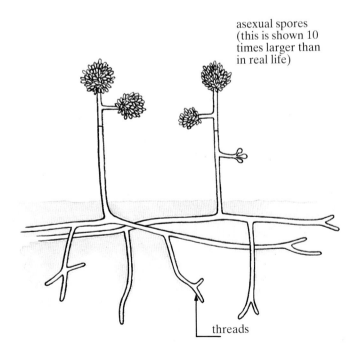

asexual spores (this is shown 10 times larger than in real life)

threads

29

FRUITING BODIES

Although the phycomycetes (see p. 28) do make fruiting bodies containing sexual spores, they are very small. The spectacular fruiting bodies that we usually think of as fungi belong to two other groups – the ascomycetes (shooting spores) and basidiomycetes (dropping spores).

The ascomycetes get their name from their flask-shaped spore containers called **asci**. It is the largest group with over 30,000 different kinds. It includes most lichens (see p. 18), microscopic forms like yeasts, mildews, and molds, as well as larger forms. In the mildews and molds the asci develop at the end of special threads. In the larger fungi, such as the cup fungi, the asci form a layer inside a cup-shaped fruiting body. In others the asci are contained in complex fruiting bodies. The ascus usually contains eight spores but yeast, one exception, produces only four. When ripe, the ascus swells up

Many Forms
The ascomycetes include many different kinds of fungi from the tiny molds and mildews to the large edible morel. Some typical kinds are shown here.

The common white *Helvella*, or saddle fungus, appears in many woods in late summer or autumn.

The rose mildew, *Sphaerotheca* species, is a common sight on garden roses.

The candle snuff fungus, *Xylaria hypoxylon*, has antler-shaped fruiting bodies about 1.2 inches high. It is found on decaying tree stumps throughout the year and is very widespread.

The eyelash fungus, *Scutellinia scutellata*, grows up to .4 inches across with long, black hairs around the edge which look like eyelashes. It grows on wet ground from spring to autumn.

Coral spot fungus, *Nectria cinnabarina*, forms pinkish or dark red fruiting bodies less than .2 inches across. It is very common and is found on decaying wood of many kinds.

with water and bursts open. The spores are shot into the air and are blown away to a new site.

The basidiomycetes also get their name from the special cell in which the spores grow – the **basidium**. The cell grows four tiny stalks with one spore on the end of each stalk. These basidia often grow on gills or in pores on the fruiting body. When ripe, the spores drop down between the gills or pores. This group contains nearly all the mushrooms we eat, and the other well-known toadstools we do not eat.

Shedding spores
Puffballs have a small hole at the top of the ball, which is full of spores. When a drop of rain hits any part of the ball, it shakes the whole fungus. The result is a smokelike puff of spores that floats away on the air. The common bird's nest fungus (pictured here) also depends on the rain. The nest-shaped fruiting body contains several "eggs" – tiny balls of spores. When the raindrop hits these "eggs" they are bounced out of the nest and travel some distance away.

Stinkhorns
When the stinkhorn, *Phallus impudicus*, first grows above ground, its top is covered with a thick slime that smells like rotting meat. Its smell attracts flies, which pick up the sticky slime and carry it to other things such as rotting plants – a good source of food for the fungus.

The shaggy ink cap
The shaggy ink cap, *Coprinus comatus*, is well named, because it turns to ink. Unlike most fungi the spores ripen from the edge of the gill first. When the spores from the edge have gone, the gills turn to liquid ink in order to leave room for the next area of spores to fall.

EDIBLE FUNGI

There are many thousands of species of fungus, and a large number are used in food, drink, medicines, and industry. In many eastern and central European countries, both fresh and dried fungi are an important food. In Finland, two to four million pounds are harvested each year. France was the first major European country to cultivate mushrooms, but now it is a thriving industry in many countries. In China and Japan, the Padi straw mushroom and the shiitaka fungus are cultivated on a large scale.

Many wild fungi can be collected and eaten, but great care must be taken to ensure that they are not poisonous. Some unusual but distinctive edible mushrooms are the

Field mushrooms
The field mushroom (*Agaricus campestris*) has an earthy smell and flavor. It always grows in grass and is white and silky with pink gills that become dark as the spores develop.

Hedgehog fungus
The hedgehog fungus (*Hydnum repandrum*) has tiny, soft, spinelike projections on the underside of the fruiting body. It is found in both deciduous and coniferous woodlands.

Giant puffballs
The giant puffball (*Langermannia gigantea*) is the size of a football and pale tan in color. It can be eaten while young and is found almost anywhere, but it is not common.

shaggy ink cap and the oyster mushroom. The former is found in fertile grasslands and like all the ink caps slowly turns to ink as the spores ripen. The oyster mushroom (see p. 9) is tasty if picked while young. One bracket fungus which is considered a delicacy in the U.S. and Germany is the sulfur polypore, or chicken of the woods, *Laetiporus sulphureus*. It grows on oak, cherry, sweet chestnut, willow, and yew.

The ceps, which have pores instead of gills, are also excellent to eat. They are often used to make canned soup. There are ceps that should not be eaten, but they have bright red gills and are rare.

Some edible fungi like the chanterelle (*Cantherellus cibarius*) and the wood blewit (*Lepista nuda*) are easily mistaken for poisonous fungi, so great care must be taken (see p. 34). Some edible fungi which are very distinctive are pictured below. However, you should never eat fungi unless they have been identified by an expert.

The cauliflower fungus
The cauliflower fungus (*Sparassis crispus*) gets its name from its appearance. It is found at the base of conifers. It is pale cream, with waxlike flesh, and is tasty to eat when young.

morel

false
morel

Horn of plenty
The horn of plenty (*Craterellus cornucopioides*) is very funnel-shaped so that the hollow extends most of the way down the stem. It is found in leaf litter in forests in August and September.

The morels
Morels (*Morchella* species) grow on grassy well-cultivated ground. In central Europe the dried fungus is an important food. The false morel should not be eaten as it is deadly poisonous.

POISONOUS FUNGI

Poisonous fungi are found throughout the world, but they are relatively rare. So far, **botanists** (people who study plants) have identified over 13,500 different mushrooms and toadstools and of these only about 20 are known to be deadly poisonous. About another 44 kinds are known to cause sickness.

There is only one way to find out if a fungus is poisonous – identify it. Folk tales say that if you cannot peel a mushroom or toadstool it is poisonous, but this is not always true – the death cap, for instance, peels quite easily and is deadly to humans when eaten. Similarly, if other animals can eat fungi safely it does not mean that humans can. Many animals can digest fungal poisons that would kill humans.

Even the saying "red spells danger" is not always true. There are at least 19 red toadstools that can be eaten safely, but two others, the fly agaric (see p. 22), and the "sickener" (see opposite) are poisonous. The fly agaric causes hallucinations (seeing and hearing things that are not real), but it rarely causes death.

Deadly poison
Very few toadstools cause death, but those that do can be fatal when even very small amounts are eaten. The deadliest toadstool is the death cap, *Amanita phalloides*.

Growth of a death cap toadstool

cap

veil

cap

ring

gills

stalk

feeding body

The "sickener"

Russula emetica, the "sickener," causes stomach cramps and sickness when eaten, as its name suggests. It is found in pine woods throughout the northern hemisphere.

Roll-brims

This brown toadstool, commonly known as the brown roll-brim, *Paxillus involutus*, is found in deciduous woodland during summer and autumn. When eaten it causes stomach cramps, dizziness, and kidney damage. It has been known to cause death.

Friend or Foe?

Look at the fungi pictured below. You will see that the different pairs are similar in some ways. However, all those on the right are harmless to humans. Those on the left are poisonous. Never assume a fungus is safe to eat. Make sure it has been accurately identified by an expert.

POISONOUS

Omphalotus olearius
■ Found in oak and chestnut woods
■ Gives off strong, unpleasant smell

Cortinarius pseudosalor
■ Found in beech and conifer woods in autumn
■ It leaves a rust-colored spore print; inedible

Amanita pantherina (panther cap)
■ Found in woodland from summer to autumn
■ Ring tears if moved

EDIBLE

Cantherellus cibarius (chanterelle)
■ Found in woodland
■ Gives off faint smell of apricots

Lepista nuda (wood blewit)
■ Found in woodland, hedgerows, and gardens in autumn
■ Has pale pink spore print

Lepiota procera (parasol mushroom)
■ Found in grassland and woods in summer and autumn
■ Movable ring

(Note: To make spore prints, see p. 28)

ANIMAL PARTNERSHIPS

As in the rest of the living world, partnerships have developed between different organisms and fungi. They form associations with trees and other higher plants (see p. 22) and with algae (see p. 18). They also form partnerships with animals. Just as some animals carry the seeds of green plants to new sites, so do they carry the spores of fungi from one place to another. Animals that eat the fruiting bodies while grazing, for example cows and deer, deposit the spores on the ground in their droppings. The spores of the stinkhorn are carried by flies, which feed on their slimy covering. Fungal spores and threads are often taken from one tree to another by wood-boring beetles. As the beetles eat the leaves or bore into the tree the fungus is deposited. The spores germinate and the threads spread throughout the tree (see p. 12).

In some cases, these partnerships are much more organized, and there are definite advantages for both partners. For example, some insects such as ants encourage the growth of fungi inside their nests. Often ants that make the walls of their nests from chewed up leaves and wood encourage the growth of a particular kind of fungus. The fungal threads make the wall stronger and the ants provide the fungus with a food source free of other competitors. All other fungi are removed so that unwanted molds do not rot the developing eggs and grubs.

Fungus gardens
Termites in the tropics of Asia and Africa build very large nests of hardened earth. They often tower up to 30 feet high. Inside there are many tunnels, some of which are specially shaped for fungus "gardens." The gardens contain the droppings of termites, and the fungus feeds on these. The worker termites feed on the fungus. Occasionally the fungus grows a giant fruiting body, with a stalk almost 6 feet high and two feet across. It looks like a giant sunshade on top of the nest.

Parasol ants

Parasol ants live in the forests of South America. They cut out pieces of leaf about .4 inches across, and carry the pieces down to their nest beneath the ground. They look as if they are carrying green parasols. The ants chew up the pieces of leaf into a pulp and place them in special underground "gardens." The ants collect the spores and threads of certain fungi and carry them down into these gardens. The threads of the feeding body grow into the pulp, and use the food to produce special swollen ends to the threads. The ants feed on these swellings and their saliva helps to nourish the fungus. The ants take out any unwanted "weeds" including other fungi, and transplant pieces of feeding body into new gardens. Young queens even carry pellets of the fungus on their flight from the nest so that they can start a new garden in the new nest.

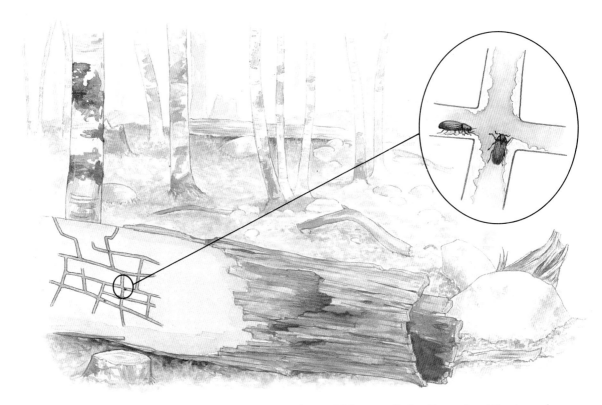

Ambrosia beetles

The ambrosia beetle makes its nest inside rotting wood. It carries into it spores of a fungus which germinate and grow on the wood. Eventually the mold forms a lining throughout the tunnels made by the beetle. The beetles tend the fungus, removing unwanted spores of other fungi. They feed on the threads and their grubs eat the spores.

INDUSTRIAL USES

Many fungi, particularly the microscopic yeasts and molds, are used a great deal in the food and drinks industry. Other fungi stain wood and are used in the furniture industry.

Bread, wine, and beer are all made with the help of yeasts. A yeast is a strange fungus (see p. 9), because it does not have threadwork like almost all other fungi. Instead, yeasts are formed of tiny oval cells, each of which buds off new cells. When there is enough water, sugar, and warmth, yeasts grow well. When there is a lot of oxygen around, the yeast will produce a gas, carbon dioxide, and water as waste products. When oxygen is in short supply, the yeast produces alcohol by a process called **fermentation**. It is these waste products that we put to good use. The carbon dioxide gas causes bread dough to rise, forming all the tiny "holes" you can see in a loaf. The alcohol produced by fermentation is used in making wine and beer. We use different strains of the yeast *Saccharomyces cerevisiae* to make bread and wine.

Natural fermentation

In nature, similar yeasts to those used in bread and wine making are found all over fruit. The "bloom" on grapes and plums is caused by millions of tiny yeast cells. When the fruit starts to rot (right), it often has a yeasty smell of wine.

Blue cheeses

Other fungi are used in the cheese-making industry. Roquefort is probably one of the most well known blue cheeses (see below). In the past, these cheeses were made by the natural action of fungi already present in the milk. Now the production is carefully controlled and only the fungus *Penicillium roquefortii* is used to produce the typical blue streaks in the cheese.

Brown oak

The beefsteak fungus or ox-tongue fungus, *Fistulina hepatica,* also stains wood. This fungus is parasitic on chestnut and oak and is usually clearly visible on the lower part of the trunk. The oak timber is stained a darker, richer color, and is known in the industry as "brown oak." It is used to make fine furniture.

Permanent colors

Some fungi stain wood permanent colors. The tiny green wood cup, *Chlorosplenium aeruginascens,* stains wood a deep blue-green. The stained wood can often be seen lying on the forest floor. Fruiting bodies are formed only rarely in this species. The wood, known as "green oak," is used to make decorative furniture.

FUNGI AND HUMANS

Fungi are all around us, and so it is not surprising that they have a great impact on our lives. In some ways they are useful "friends," but in others, they cause great damage.

Fungi cause decay, so they tend to attack any food supply. When this is our stored food, ready for future use, it is very costly. To try and prevent this from happening, we store food in a way that is unfavorable for the growth of fungi. We remove the water that they need by storing foods like cookies dry, and sealed in a tin. We remove the warmth fungi need by keeping food in refrigerators and freezers. To be effective, the temperatures must be low enough to prevent fungal growth. A third possibility is to give food a very small dose of radiation. This would kill any fungal spores on the food. It would be dangerous to treat food in this way if it had begun to decay even slightly as poisons might have been produced by the growing fungi. These poisons could make people ill when the food was eaten.

The parasitic fungi that cause disease and death cost us a great deal. Wheat rust and ergot of rye have caused great financial loss, as well as suffering because of famine from crop failure. The potato blight that caused a famine in Ireland in the 1860s killed thousands and caused many more people to emigrate.

Dry rot
As well as decaying our food, fungi also attack our homes. All the wood in our buildings has to be kept as dry as possible otherwise it might be attacked by the dry rot fungus. Although this fungus needs water to germinate and start growing, once it has started it produces its own water. When it is well developed, it can pass over metal, concrete, or any other nonfood object, to reach a food supply beyond. We combat it by painting wood and using preservatives, but it still causes very expensive damage.

Fermented foods

Without yeasts, we would not have bread, yogurt, some cheeses, wine, or beer. We would not have hard cider from apples, sake from rice, or rum from molasses.

On the positive side, we could not survive if fungi did not decay the dead material that is produced daily. The dead bodies of animals and plants would not rot away as quickly, and would soon prove an enormous problem. The materials locked up in them, which are essential for the growth of plants, would be lost. Once plants were in short supply, animals and humans would soon be hungry. Lichens give us the benefit of being able to measure pollution, which gives us the chance to try and correct our mistakes. Mycorrhizae enable us to grow trees on poor soil and to grow better crops. Many orchids would be missing, too. Without antibiotics, humans would still be dying from diseases we hardly ever hear of today.

Fungal food

Without fungi we would not have an excellent source of food. Both China and Japan grow fungi for food, and have probably been doing so for over 1,000 years. In the mid-1970s the annual weight of mushrooms grown in the world was nearly 275,000 tons. It is a very economical crop to grow, and takes up little space. One acre can produce over 80 tons of mushrooms a year.

SLIME MOLDS

Slime molds are very unusual as they have both animal and fungal features. They have been studied for over 200 years, and no one is quite sure to which group they belong. Some people think they should be put with the fungi and give them the name myxomycetes (slime mold); others put them in the animal kingdom and call them mycetozoa (fungus animals). Myxomycetes is the term often used, although, as they do not have a feeding body like most fungi, they are probably not closely related to fungi.

The animal-like stage of slime molds is a creeping, feeding stage called the **plasmodium**. It is not made up of cells, but is just a mass of **protoplasm** (living jellylike material) containing **nuclei** (the control center of living cells). Unlike fungi it does not have a cell wall. Plasmodia live in dark, damp places, for example among dead leaves, inside logs, and even on fungi. They move and feed like a simple animal called an amoeba. That is, they feed by flowing around the food and enclosing it in a tiny sac. The food is then digested and the unwanted remains are emptied outside.

Once the slime mold has taken in enough food, it comes out onto the surface. At this stage it becomes stationary and needs light. It begins to make large numbers of fruiting bodies like a fungus. The spore containers or fruiting bodies usually have an outer "coat" and often have a stalk. Inside the coat, among the spores, are hairs. These hairs vary in shape and size and are used to identify slime molds.

life size x 20

Best-known slime mold
Perhaps the most well-known and certainly the most studied slime mold is *Physarum polycephalum*. It can be grown, fairly easily, in the laboratory and has been used to find out how slime molds live.

Slime Molds Everywhere!

There are about 500 slime molds and most of them are found throughout the world; 350 kinds are found in the U.S. A few appear to be limited to tropical and subtropical areas, and yet others are found only in the montane or melting snow regions. Here are five common examples.

life size x 12

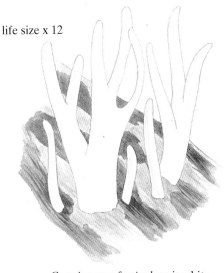

life size

Lycogala epidendron is an unstalked species with fruiting bodies up to .5 inches across. It is rose-pink when young, and ages to a yellowish brown.

Ceratiomyxa fruticulosa is white and shaped like a tiny column or pillar. Each pillar is covered with microscopic spores, which have hairlike threads.

life size x 12

Arcyria cinera is gray and shaped like a cylinder that narrows at the top. It has a stalk and grows to a height of about .2 inches.

life size x 4

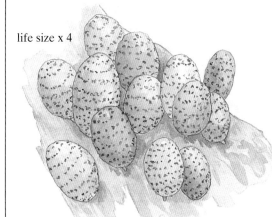

life size

Arcyria denudata have stalked spore capsules up to .25 inches in height. They look like short, fat balloons crowded together. They are red when young, aging to brownish or brownish-green.

Fuligo septica is usually yellow and quite large, growing up to 8 inches across. They come in a variety of colors – white, yellow, orange, brick-red, brown, and violet – but these forms are less common.

GLOSSARY

ABSORB – The process by which soluble food products are taken up by plant or animal cells.

ALGA (plural algae) – Simple green plants that have no root, stem, or flower.

ANTIBIOTIC – A chemical made by a fungus which is poisonous to some other organisms and is useful in medicine to fight infections.

ASCUS (plural asci) – Flask-shaped spore containers.

BACTERIUM (plural bacteria) – A microscopic organism.

BASIDIUM (plural basidia) – A spore-producing cell which has its spores (almost always four) on the end of the cell.

BOTANISTS – People who study plants.

CHLOROPHYLL – The green pigment of plants that absorbs energy from light to make food by photosynthesis.

DORMANT – An inactive or resting stage before growth begins.

ENZYMES – Chemicals that can break down, or digest, animal and plant materials.

FEEDING BODY – The threads of the fungus, connected to each other, which have spread throughout its food supply.

FERMENTATION – A process in which yeasts break down sugar, in the absence of oxygen gas, to produce alcohol and carbon dioxide.

FRUITING BODY – The part of the fungus that makes the spores.

HYPHA (plural hyphae) – A fungal thread.

INDICATOR – A substance that is a different color in acid and alkaline solutions.

MYCELIUM (plural mycelia) – A feeding body.

MYCOLOGISTS – People who study fungi.

MYCORRHIZA (plural mycorrhizae) – The swollen roots formed by plant roots and fungal threads living together in a partnership.

NUCLEUS – The central part of a living cell which controls its activities. It also contains the genetic material that carries information on the structure of the cell.

ORGANISM – Any living thing – a plant, animal, fungus, or bacterium.

PARASITES – Organisms that grow on living plants and animals.

PHOTOSYNTHESIS – The process in green plants that turns carbon dioxide and water into sugars and oxygen using the energy in sunlight.

PLASMODIUM – The creeping and feeding stage of a slime mold (myxomycete).

PROTOPLASM – A living jellylike material.

PUPA – The stage between a caterpillar and an adult insect.

RHIZOMORPH – The black "boot lace" strands found in some fungi (for example, the honey fungus) that are formed from several threads clinging together.

SAPROPHYTE – An organism that lives and feeds on dead plant and animal remains.

SPORANGIA – A balloon-shaped spore container.

SPORE – A reproductive body that will grow into a new fungus.

SYMBIOSIS – A symbiotic relationship is one in which two different organisms live together, usually with some benefit for each other.

XYLEM – The tubes in a plant which carry water and mineral salts from the roots to all parts of the plant.

YEASTS – Yeasts are single-celled fungi that make new cells by budding.

FURTHER READING

For children:
Mushrooms by Sylvia A. Johnson; Lerner Publications, 1982.
For adults:
The Fungi of Our Mouldy Earth (A Compilation), by Bridge W. Cooke; Lubrecht & Cramer, 1986.
How to Know the Mosses & Liverworts by Henry S. Conrad; Wm. C. Brown, 1979.
Lichens: An Illustrated Guide by Frank Dobson; Richmond Publishing, 1981.
Mushrooms & Other Fungi by Aurel Dermek; Arco, 1985.

SPECIES IN THIS BOOK

Ascomycetes
Bread and beer yeast (*Saccharomyces cerevisiae*)
Candle snuff (*Xylaria hypoxylon*)
Coral spot (*Nectria cinnabarina*)
Ergot of rye (*Claviceps purpurea*)
Eyelash fungus (*Scutellinia scutellata*)
False morel (*Gyromitra esculenta*)
Green wood cup (*Chlorosplenium aeruginascens*)
Morels (*Morchella* species)
Moldy hay mold (*Aspergillus* species)
Nut and grain mold (*Aspergillus flavus*)
Penicillium notatum
Penicillium roquefortii
Peziza repanda
Rose mildew (*Sphaerotheca* species)
Saddle fungus (*Helvella* species)
Scarlet caterpillar fungus (*Cordyceps militaris*)
Streptomyces griseus

Basidiomycetes
Asterophora species
Beefsteak (*Fistulina hepatica*)
Birch polypore (*Piptoporus betulinus*)
Bird's nest, common (*Crucibulum laeve*)
Black rust of wheat (*Puccinia graminis*)
Boletus parasiticus
Boletus portenosus
Brown roll-brim (*Paxillus involutus*)
Cauliflower mushroom (*Sparassis crispus*)
Chanterelle (*Cantherellus cibarius*)
Chicken of the woods or sulfur polypore
   (*Laetiporus sulphureus*)
Cortinarius pseudosalor
Death cap (*Amanita phalloides*)
Dry rot (*Serpula lacrymans*)
Earth ball (*Scleroderma* species)
Field mushroom (*Agaricus campestris*)
Fly agaric (*Amanita muscaria*)
Giant puffball (*Langermannia gigantea*)
Hedgehog fungus (*Hydnum repandrum*)
Honey fungus (*Armillaria mellea*)
Horn of plenty (*Craterellus cornucopioides*)
Ink cap (*Coprinus niveus*)
Omphalotus olearius
Ox-tongue fungus (*Fistulina hepatica*)

Oyster mushroom (*Pleurotus ostreatus*)
Panther cap (*Amanita pantherina*)
Parasol mushroom (*Lepiota procera*)
Shaggy ink cap (*Coprinus comatus*)
Sickener (*Russula emetica*)
Slippery jack (*Suillus luteus*)
Stinkhorn (*Phallus impudicus*)
Suillus granulatus
Verdigris agaric (*Stropharia aeruginosa*)
Wood blewit (*Lepista nuda*)

Fungi imperfecti
Botrytus mold
Dactyella bembicodes
Epidermophyton species
Fusarium wilts
Microsporum species
Trichophyton species

Phycomycetes
Black bread mold (*Rhizopus stolonifera*)
Downy mildew of hops (*Pseudoperanospera
   humuli*)
Entomophthora muscae
Fish mold (*Saprolegnia* species)
Pilobus kleinii
Potato blight (*Phytophthora infestans*)
Potato wart disease (*Synchytrium endobioticum*)

Lichens
Hypogymnia physodes
Iceland moss (*Cetraria islandica*)
Lecanora conizaeoides
Lepraria incana
Map lichen (*Rhizocarpon geographicum*)
Parmelia saxatilis
Reindeer moss (*Cladonia rangiferina*)
Roccella species
Stag's horn (*Evernia prunastri*)
Usnea subfloridana

Myxomycetes (Slime molds)
Arcyria cinera
Arcyria denudata
Ceratiomyxa fruticulosa
Fuligo septica
Lycogala epidendron
Physarum polycephalum

INDEX

mildews 12, 14, 29, 30
monterrey pine 22
Morchella species 33
morels 30, 33
mosses 6
molds 8, 9, 10, 12, 14, 16, 29, 30, 36
mushrooms 8, 31, 32, 34, 41
mycelium 8
mycetozoa 42
mycorrhizae 18, 22, 23, 25, 26, 41
myxomycetes 42

N
Nectria cinnabarina 30
nematodes 17, 29
nitrates 11, 22
nitrogen 10
nuclei 42
nutrients 10, 11

O
Omphalotus olearius 35
orchids 24-25, 41
organism 8
ox-tongue fungus 39
oyster mushroom 8, 33

P
Padi straw mushroom 32
panther cap 35
parasites 12, 16, 25
parasol ants 37
parasol mushroom 35
Parmelia saxatilis 21
Paxillus involutus 35
Penicillium notatum 27
Penicillium roquefortii 39
Peziza repanda 11
Phallus impudicus 31
phosphates 11, 22
photosynthesis 18, 24
phycomycetes 6, 28, 29, 30
Physarum polycephalum 42
Phytophthora infestans 14, 29
Pilobus species 11
Pinus radiata 22
Piptoporus betulinus 12

plasmodium 42
Pleurococcus viridis 20
Pleurotus ostreatus 8
podocarpus 23
potato blight 14, 29, 40
potato wart 29
protoplasm 42
Pseudoperanospera humuli 14
pteridophytes 6
Puccinia graminis 15
puffballs 31

R
reindeer moss 21
Rhizocarpon geographicum 19
rhizomorphs 13
Rhizopus stolonifera 29
ringworm 16
Roccella 21
Roquefort cheese 39
rose mildew 30
rotifers 17
Russula 27
Russula emetica 35
rusts 12, 14-15, 40
rye 15, 40

S
Saccharomyces cerevisiae 26, 38
saddle fungus 30
Saint Anthony's fire 15
Saprolegnia 16, 29
saprophytes 10, 11, 16
scarlet caterpillar fungus 17
Scleroderma 27
Scutellinia scutellata 30
Serpula lacrymans 16
shaggy ink cap 31, 33
shiitaka fungus 32
"sickener" 34-35
silver leaf disease 14
slime molds 6, 42-43
slippery jack 22
smuts 14-15
soredia 20
Sparassis crispus 33
Spaerotheca species 30
sporangia 29

spore prints 28
stag's horn 19
stinkhorn 31, 36
Streptomyces 26
Streptomyces griseus 14
streptomycin 14, 27
Stropharia aeruginosa 10
sucrose 11, 22
Suillus granulatus 22
Suillus luteus 22
sulfur dioxide 20
sulfur polypore 33
symbiotic relationship 18, 22, 26
Synchytrium endobioticum 29

T
termites 36
toadstools 8, 10, 11, 31, 34
toxins 26
Trichophyton 16

U
Usnea subfloridana 21

V
verdigris agaric 10

W
wheat 15, 40
wood blewit 33, 35

X
Xylaria hypoxylon 30
xylem 12

Y
yeasts 9, 26, 30, 38, 41